anythink

D0933543

Creative Writing
in 5 Simple Steps

Write
Fantasy
Fiction
in 5 Simple Steps

Laura Lee McKay

Enslow Publishers, Inc.
40 Industrial Road
Box 398
Berkeley Heights, NJ 07922
USA

http://www.enslow.com

For Josie

Copyright © 2013 by Laura Lee McKay

All rights reserved.

No part of this book may be reproduced by any means
without the written permission of the publisher.

Library of Congress Cataloging-in-Publication Data

McKay, Laura Lee.
  Write fantasy fiction in 5 simple steps / Laura Lee McKay.
      p. cm.— (Creative writing in 5 simple steps)
  Includes bibliographical references and index.
  Summary: "Divides the creative writing process into five steps, from inspiration to publishable story, and
includes in-depth treatment of the fantasy fiction genre with writing prompts"—Provided by publisher.
  ISBN 978-0-7660-3834-9
  1. English language—Composition and exercises—Study and teaching (Middle school)—Juvenile literature.
2. Creative writing—Juvenile literature. I. Title.
  LB1631.M3945 2012
  808'.0420712—dc22
                                    2010037973

Future editions:
Paperback ISBN 978-1-4644-0098-8
ePUB ISBN 978-1-4645-1005-2
PDF ISBN 978-1-4646-1005-9

Printed in the United States of America

032012 Lake Book Manufacturing, Inc., Melrose Park, IL

10 9 8 7 6 5 4 3 2

To Our Readers: We have done our best to make sure all Internet Addresses in this book were active
and appropriate when we went to press. However, the author and the publisher have no control over and
assume no liability for the material available on those Internet sites or on other Web sites they may link to.
Any comments or suggestions can be sent by e-mail to comments@enslow.com or to the address on the back
cover.

Every effort has been made to locate all copyright holders of material used in this book. If any errors or
omissions have occurred, corrections will be made in future editions of this book.

♻ Enslow Publishers, Inc., is committed to printing our books on recycled paper. The paper in every book
contains 10% to 30% post-consumer waste (PCW). The cover board on the outside of each book contains
100% PCW. Our goal is to do our part to help young people and the environment too!

Cover and Illustration Credits: Shutterstock.com

Contents

Book Key

Keeping a Journal

On the Web

Genre History

Fun Fact

Check It Out!

Writer's Block

Here's an Idea!

Your Assignment

Organizer

Daydreaming

Step 1

Start With an Idea

One afternoon in 1990, an aspiring writer named J. K. Rowling was stuck on a long train journey from Manchester, England, to London. She was bored until the image of a boy wizard suddenly popped into her mind. Because she didn't have a pen with her, she continued to let her mind wander, deciding what she wanted to write:

> . . . *I simply sat and thought, for four (delayed train) hours, and all the details bubbled up in my brain, and this scrawny, black-haired, bespectacled boy who didn't know he was a wizard became more and more real to me.*[1]

As the years passed, Rowling wrote every day, every chance she could find, about her boy wizard until she finally finished *Harry Potter and the Sorcerer's Stone*.

Rowling's experiences prove that you never know when and where inspiration will strike. It could happen on the morning bus ride to school, while listening to a song on an iPod, or in a dream you had while taking an afternoon nap. If you work hard like Rowling did, you can end up with a fantastic piece of writing.

What Is Fantasy?

Rowling's Harry Potter series is an excellent example of the fantasy genre. Fantasy is a fun genre to read and write because you can create new worlds, people who have magical powers, and animals with unusual qualities. If you enjoy stories about wizards and witches, time travel, talking animals, fairies, and trolls, then fantasy is the perfect way to express yourself. Your characters—whether they are the protagonist, villain, or supporting characters—can be as outrageous or as lifelike as you want, as long as they are believable within the context of your story. Anything you can imagine, from making friends with a dragon to moving through parallel universes, can become real to your readers if you write effectively.

Fantasy is important because it lets us imagine ourselves in all kinds of difficult, often dangerous, situations. We are then inspired to use creative ways to overcome those challenges. Fantasy is also a way to explore problems that everyone goes through in real life. Percy Jackson, in the Percy Jackson and the Olympians series, is like any other teenager who has trouble relating to his dad. In Percy's case, his father happens to be the Greek god of the sea, Poseidon. Fantasy can also be an interesting way to turn negatives into positives. Again using Percy as an example, he and the other demigod children sometimes have ADHD and dyslexia, which can hurt them in their ordinary lives. It helps them when they are battling monsters, though, because they think differently than regular mortals. Fantasy helps us look at lots of things differently. One of the things we learn is that different can be good.

Writing can be scary, but basically, it means making choices and exploring options. For example, if you choose to have a character who is an orphan, he or she will have different feelings about family than another character who comes from a large family. Harry and Ron Weasley, from the Harry Potter series, are good examples. Think about how their family situations influence their behavior, and you'll see what an important choice that one thing can be. This book discusses some of the choices you need to make when writing a fantasy short story or novel, or even a series, and how those choices determine the course of your fiction. It's a lot easier than you might think if you break it down into steps. Just focus on one thing at a time, and you'll be led to your next choice. Before you know it, you'll have a completed work of fantasy fiction to show off to your friends and family.

What Interests You?

The first step is to decide what you want to write about. Are you interested in creating another land, for example, like Oz? Or do you want to set your story in the "real" world but have it be about unusual people? An example is Harry Potter, who lives in an ordinary English suburb but attends a school for wizards. The sorts of things you take an interest in during your everyday life can inspire you. If you really like animals, perhaps you could write about a talking animal that helps humans defeat an evil invader. Or if you are interested in history, you could choose to set your story in a time period that intrigues you, such as Colonial America, and have your protagonist travel back in time.

Famous Fantasies

The following are some of the more famous fantasy books written. If you have not already done so, go to your local library and check them out!

The Wonderful Wizard of Oz by L. Frank Baum (1900), followed by thirteen more books in the Oz series.

The Story of Doctor Dolittle (1920) by Hugh Lofting, followed by eleven more books in the Doctor Dolittle series.

The Hobbit by J. R. R. Tolkien (1937).

The Gremlins by Roald Dahl (1943).

The Wind on the Moon by Eric Linklater (1944).

The Lion, the Witch, and the Wardrobe by C. S. Lewis (1950), followed by six more books in the Chronicles of Narnia series.

The Borrowers by Mary Norton (1952), followed by four more books in the Borrowers series.

The Fellowship of the Rings by J. R. R. Tolkien (1954), followed by two more books in the Lord of the Rings trilogy.

A Wrinkle in Time by Madeleine L'Engle (1962), followed by three more books in the Time Quartet.

Charlie and the Chocolate Factory by Roald Dahl (1964), followed by the sequel *Charlie and the Great Glass Elevator*.

The Owl Service by Alan Garner (1967).

The Last Unicorn by Peter S. Beagle (1968).

Watership Down by Richard Adams (1972).

The Princess Bride by William Goldman (1973).

Tuck Everlasting by Natalie Babbitt (1975).

Bridge to Terabithia by Katherine Paterson (1977).

The Blue Sword by Robin McKinley (1982).

Dragons of Autumn Twilight by Margaret Weis and Tracy Hickman (1984), followed by many more books in the Dragonlance series, often by other authors.

Catwings by Ursula K. LeGuin (1988), followed by three more books in the Catwings Collection.

Truckers by Terry Pratchett (1990), followed by two more books in the Bromeliad Trilogy.

The Golden Compass by Philip Pullman (1995), followed by two more books in the His Dark Materials series.

No One Noticed the Cat by Anne McCaffrey (1996).

Harry Potter and the Sorcerer's Stone by J. K. Rowling (1998), followed by six more books in the Harry Potter series.

Skellig by David Almond (1998).

Stardust by Neil Gaiman (1999).

Artemis Fowl by Eoin Colfer (2001), followed by seven more books in the Artemis Fowl series.

Coraline by Neil Gaiman (2002).

Into the Wild by Erin Hunter (2003), first in the Warriors series which consists of four series, with six books in each.

Eragon by Christopher Paolini (2003), followed by three more books in the Inheritance Cycle.

Inkheart by Cornelia Funke (2003), followed by two more books in the Inkworld series.

Dragon Rider by Cornelia Funke (2004).

Maximum Ride: The Angel Experiment by James Patterson (2005), followed by seven more books in the Maximum Ride series.

Disney After Dark by Ridley Pearson (2005), followed by four more books in the Kingdom Keepers series, with a total of seven books planned.

The Book Thief by Markus Zusak (2005).

The Lightning Thief by Rick Riordan (2005), followed by four more books in the Percy Jackson and the Olympians series.

You can even create a protagonist that isn't a living being, such as a robot or a wooden puppet shaped like a little boy. Do you enjoy fairy tales? Try to tell a fairy tale in an offbeat way that hasn't been seen before. Using your other interests in your writing will help you complete your project and create something that will truly interest your readers. Don't pick something only because you think it will sell well. If your work doesn't hold your interest, it won't hold your readers' interest either.

Fantasy does not have to be about magical animals or countries populated by munchkins, however. It can, and often does, deal with very real subjects, but from an unusual perspective. For example, Markus Zusak's *The Book Thief* is set in Germany during World War II, and the protagonist is a young girl growing up amid the horrors of the Holocaust. What makes the book fantasy is the narrator, Death, who can describe things in ways that ordinary people can't.

Along with your interests, you will need to use your own experiences to help you. Rowling relates that after her mother died, her grief enabled her to write more realistically about what Harry was feeling, and that his feelings about his parents "had become much deeper, much more real."[2] This is when she was able to write the chapter about the mirror of Erised, in which Harry sees his dead parents as if they were alive. On her Web site, Rowling says that this became her favorite chapter of *Harry Potter and the Sorcerer's Stone*. Even if you have had unhappy or difficult things happen to you, you can use them in your writing. You can also use more ordinary things to help you with your writing. According to a post on Shurtagal.com, Christopher Paolini used his own color blindness as the basis for the way the dragon Saphira sees everything in blue.[3]

You Can Do It, Too!

Christopher Paolini, the author of the Inheritance Cycle, was just fifteen years old when he began writing *Eragon*. According to his Web site, Paolini's "love for the magic of stories led him to craft a novel that he would enjoy reading."[4] His success is a great reminder that inspiration knows no age boundaries. If you write something that you would like to read, it will probably interest others, too. Paolini's Web site also reports that his physical surroundings, the Beartooth Mountains near his home in Paradise Valley, Montana, were the inspiration for the amazing scenery of *Eragon*. So be observant about your everyday life. You never know what will inspire you to write something fantastic.

For more inspiring stories, browse the Internet. You'll find articles from different writers about what interests them, why they write, and how they find subjects for their stories. Start keeping a journal of ideas for stories, words you learn, characters you think of, books you want to read, your favorite writers—anything that motivates you.

One of the great things about fantasy is that you get to make up your own rules. There don't have to be the usual limits of time, space, cause and effect, or even gravity. As long as you are consistent and make it believable to the reader, your imagination is your only limit. Consistency is a key element of effective fantasy. It's a good idea to begin thinking now about the rules governing your story so you don't violate them. For example, if you've decided that cats can talk but not dogs, don't have Rover speaking up in the middle of the story. That might seem like a silly example, but do examine all angles of the choices you make as you go through the steps in this book. Whatever your choices are, you'll have to make sure that your characters look, act, talk, dress, and think according to the rules you create. Again, there are many things to consider, but if you make your choices with conviction and stick to them with consistency throughout your writing, you'll create something really fun for your readers.

What Do You Dream About?

What are your favorite daydreams? Do you like to imagine yourself flying or learning to use magic? Perhaps being invisible and catching robbers? Using your ideas journal, keep track of your daydreams and see how you can turn them into fantasy fiction. Do you want to create a whole world in which cats are the rulers and dogs the servants? What makes you laugh and cry? What are you afraid of? These are the things that will make your world intriguing because you will be able to write about them with conviction. Record your dreams, both nighttime and daytime, and see where they lead you. Write some paragraphs or short stories about your dreams. Don't worry about them being polished yet, just start writing.

Step 2

Gather Story Elements

There are many choices to make when deciding who your protagonist, villain, and supporting characters will be. You want to make sure that they are compelling people who make your readers curious about what happens to them. Rick Riordan, the author of the Percy Jackson and the Olympians series, offers a helpful checklist to use for each of your characters. Things to consider include age; physical characteristics, such as height, hair color, and strength; things they are good at; and things they are bad at. An example of a physical trait adding flavor to a story is the bright red hair of the Weasley family in the Harry Potter series. Even Harry's big, round glasses make him that much more interesting.

Even though they live in a fantastic world that you have created, your characters need to be believable. They can't be completely powerful or have unrealistic flaws. Characters should be three-dimensional, which means that they have good and bad qualities. Even a house elf needs to be realistic, and even Voldemort has weaknesses, despite how powerful he is. Try to craft positive characters you would like to be friends with if you met them in real life. And your villains can have personality traits that you find scary, too. One of the great things about fantasy fiction is that it allows us to confront scary ideas and situations in a safe way.

Doing Your Research

Doing research is a lot of fun. You get to read books by different authors and discover what about their writing styles and stories appeals to you. Go online and find authors you haven't read before and find out what other people your age like or dislike about them. Keep track of them in your ideas journal. While you are reading their books, however, be careful that you do not steal any ideas. That is called plagiarism. Although it is okay to be inspired by another author—for example, you like Harry Potter so much that you want to write about wizards—it would be plagiarism if you copied J. K. Rowling's ideas. Remember, never take ideas from another writer without giving him or her credit.

To learn more about fantasy fiction, and the many authors who can inspire you, search the Internet and read some of the more popular fantasy books. Don't forget your school library or the local branch of your public library! Browse through the fantasy section and see what catches your eye. The librarian can help you find new titles in addition to the ones already discussed.

Who Are Your Characters?

When thinking about your characters, pay as much attention to the "sidekicks" and minor characters as you do to the lead. Fantasy rarely involves a "lone wolf" type of character who acts solely on his or her own without the help of others. The lead character is almost always supported by friends, teachers, and family members. You want to make sure that their strengths and weaknesses fit together well. For example, Harry could never have gotten through the traps leading to the Sorcerer's Stone without Ron and Hermione. It was Ron's skill at chess that enabled them to cross the giant chessboard, while Hermione's aptitude for logic helped uncover the right potion in the last challenge. Harry's passion and bravery help Ron and Hermione face their fears throughout the series.

If you have lively minor characters, such as Dobby from Harry Potter or Chiron from the Percy Jackson series, your readers will have more fun along the way. Plus you'll be able to relate vital information without always relying on your main characters. Sometimes it helps to think of your story as a giant rug with a picture on it, and each character as a thread running through it. You want them to weave together, displaying lots of color, so it creates a vivid, enjoyable picture when seen as a whole.

The Quest

Most fantasies involve a quest, whether it is walking along a yellow brick road or searching for knowledge during seven years of schooling. An important thing to decide is what you want your characters to learn on their journey. They need to be traveling or searching for a specific reason, not just wandering around for the sake of it. In addition to the goal (finding Horcruxes, rescuing a friend, tracking down the Ra'zac, etc.), your characters need to learn and grow during their quest. It may be that they need to learn how to use their powers, like Meggie from *Inkheart,* or how to control their emotions, as often happens to Harry Potter.

A journey is also a useful plot device to allow characters to learn about their destiny. For example, in Christopher Paolini's *Eragon,* it is not until Eragon has been to a slave market that he decides to join the Varden, the group fighting the evil King Galbatorix. Although his companions had told Eragon that he should rise up against the tyrant, it wasn't until he experienced something firsthand that he could accept their advice. At the beginning of *The Amber Spyglass,* Will realizes that he must make choices for himself during his journey and that his choices have serious consequences:

> *Will considered what to do. When you choose one way out of many, all the ways you don't take are snuffed out like candles, as if they'd never existed. At the moment all Will's choices existed at once. But to keep them all in existence meant doing nothing. He had to choose, after all.[1]*

By the end of a quest, the characters are more confident and wiser, even if they have been hurt or lost friends. Make sure that each part of their journey contributes to their growth as people. If readers can imagine what they would do if they were in your hero's place, then you have done your job as a writer.

One of the scariest things about writing is that first blank page. Whether you use a computer or handwrite your story, it can be difficult to begin. What would be a good opening line to hook the reader? Should you start with a detailed description or lively dialogue? Don't worry! Just get your thoughts down on paper, however they come. You can revise and edit them later, as we see in Step 4. The important thing is to begin. No one expects you to be perfect when you first start, so just write, write, write.

What Time Is It?

One choice you will have to make as you write your fantasy story is when it will be set. Do you want to set your story in the current day or at some point in the past? As with all choices, there are pluses and minuses to what you pick. Think about the consequences of your choice. For example, if your story is set now, your characters will have access to such things as cell phones and computers. Then again, if it is set in the past, they can meet historical people, such as Abraham Lincoln or Cleopatra. They can be involved in events from long ago, such as when Christopher Columbus discovered America or when dinosaurs were alive. Pick a time that works best for the goals you are trying to achieve and the message you want to get across.

Practice Makes Perfect

There is a genre called "fan fiction," in which you write stories using characters that were created by someone else. The characters could be from movies, TV shows, comic books, and, of course, novels. It's like paying tribute to the original author's ideas but putting your own spin on them. Crafting fan fiction is a fun and useful way to practice writing. The characters and the world are already there for you to play with; all you need to do is think up new challenges for them. Some fan-fiction writers even create crossover stories where characters from one series visit another author's universe.

To learn more about fan fiction, search for fan-fiction sites on the Web. The Harry Potter series seems to have inspired more fan fiction than any other fantasy series. Some Potter fan fiction can be found at MuggleNet. Browse through these sites or find your own for your favorite characters and authors. Write a fan-fiction short story using already established characters and get the opinions of your friends who also like those characters. Were you true to the characters and able to come up with fresh things to say? Were you able to create new challenges for them?

Step 3

Organize Your Story

One of the choices you need to make in this step is how you are going to narrate your story. There are two basic types of narration: first person and third person. In first-person narration, you tell the story through the eyes of your protagonist, as if he or she is directly reporting events. This is also called the "I" style of narration. Here's an example from *The Lightning Thief,* in which Percy talks about his learning challenges:

> *I have moments like that a lot, when my brain falls asleep or something, and the next thing I know I've missed something, as if a puzzle piece fell out of the universe and left me staring at the blank place behind it. The school counselor told me this was part of the ADHD, my brain misinterpreting things.*
> *I wasn't so sure.*[1]

How to Tell Your Story

First-person narration is useful if you want to tell the story solely from your protagonist's point of view. It allows you to relay his or her feelings and thoughts directly to the reader. Because of its intimacy, it can allow the reader to pretend that he or she is the hero.

However, it will be more difficult for you to relate how your other characters are feeling and what their experiences are. For example, Percy can tell you what he is feeling, but his friends cannot because Percy is narrating the story. All you know about them is what they tell Percy and what Percy tells you.

Where Are the Parents?

Have you ever noticed that few protagonists in fantasy fiction have complete families? Harry's parents were killed when he was a baby, Meggie's mother has been missing for years, Lyra's parents are both absent from her life, Percy's father, Poseidon, is largely absent from his life . . . the list goes on and on. Why do you think this is? What can be gained, as far as your protagonist's development, by his or her having a difficult family background? In Meggie's case, being without her mother for so many years has made her extremely close to her father. When he is kidnapped, she is desperate to help him. Harry's being an orphan gives him a vulnerability to which readers respond.

There are advantages to having a whole family, however. In *Inkspell* and *Inkdeath*, after Meggie's parents have been reunited, their closeness gives Meggie strength. Ron Weasley's family is an important part of who he is, and they contribute to Harry's growth throughout the years. Think carefully about the families of your characters. Even if they are not important characters, consider what their absence or presence will add to your story.

Think carefully about what your first-person narrator tells the reader during your story, and make sure it is something that your narrator can know. Unless he or she can read minds, the narrator can't know everything.

In third-person narration, often referred to as "omniscient narration," it's like an all-seeing outsider is telling the story and reporting the feelings and experiences of all the characters. Although you usually focus on your protagonist, you can tell the story from more than his or her single point of view. Omniscient narration can tell you everything but at a distance.

This type of narration is useful because you can switch back and forth between the points of view of different characters. For part of one chapter, you can describe how your protagonist feels as he or she undergoes a challenge and then switch to what the sidekick is thinking. Although omniscient narration doesn't have the same "right here, right now" feeling of first-person narration, you can describe the feelings and experiences of all your characters equally. Here's an example of third-person narration from *Inkspell,* when Dustfinger is scouting the inn where Mo and Resa are being held prisoner:

There were guards outside the stable where the prisoners had been shut up, four guards, but they didn't notice him. They were staring into the night, their faces bored, hands on their sword hilts, looking longingly again and again at the lighted windows opposite. Loud, drunken voices came from the inn—and then the sound of a lute, its strings well plucked, followed by singing in a curiously strained voice. Ah, so the Piper was back from Ombra, too, and singing one of his songs, drunk with blood and the intoxication of killing. The presence of the man with the silver nose was yet another reason why he had to stay out of sight. Meggie and Farid were waiting behind the stables, as agreed, but they were arguing in such loud voices that Dustfinger came up behind the boy and put his hand over his mouth.[2]

Although this passage is told from Dustfinger's point of view, because it is third-person narration, the author can tell the reader how different characters are feeling. If it were in first-person narration, Dustfinger would be guessing about what was going on.

There are variations on these types of narration. For example, in *The Book Thief*, the first-person narrator is Death, who describes his feelings and experiences while he is discussing Liesel Meminger. Even though Liesel is the book's protagonist, she is not the first-person narrator. Until you've had a lot of practice, it's best to stick to more basic storytelling and use either first-person or omniscient narration. Try them both as you begin writing your story so you can decide which one tells your story the best. Write a couple paragraphs in both styles and see which one reveals your characters more vividly.

 ## Outlines and Maps

Now that you have some ideas about your world, such as who lives in it and what its rules are, organize your thoughts with an outline. Write down the progression of your story, where it starts, what twists it will take, and how you want it to end. What do you want each character to learn? What qualities will they have at the end that they didn't have at the beginning?

A fun way of organizing your world, especially if it is completely make-believe, is to draw a map. J. R. R. Tolkien, the brilliant author of *The Hobbit* and the Lord of the Rings series, was famous for his incredibly detailed and realistic maps of the world that he created, Middle-earth. Not only do maps help readers after the story is written, they also help the authors follow the geography of their lands while they are writing. It will be a great help to have a map so you can keep track of where the desert is located, the forest, the jungle, the islands, etc. Or if you have a really big building, like Hogwarts, it could be helpful to draw a diagram of it.

Rules, Rules, Rules

There are many conventions in fantasy fiction—that is, rules that have evolved over time that authors frequently use. Conventions are common-sense rules for worlds, characters, and situations not usually governed by common sense. For example, dragons can usually only converse with their riders or other magical beings, and vampires cannot come out during the daylight. Conventions are what "everyone knows" about certain things. They give readers a headstart and help authors create believable characters. Using the journal you started in Step 1 and the books you researched in Step 2, keep track of fantasy conventions you run across. How do they help the story you're reading, or not? How could you apply them to your own story? What are the advantages or disadvantages of doing things differently? For example, how does it hurt or help your vampire if he or she can be seen in a mirror?

Describing the Beasties

If a work of fantasy is truly effective, you can get a mental picture of what the author is describing, even if it is something that he or she created. Readers will be sucked into the imaginary world and feel like they are accompanying the main character on his or her magical journey, seeing, touching, hearing, smelling, and tasting everything that he or she does.

Being able to describe what you have thought up is very important and so basic that it is easy to overlook. You might take for granted that everyone knows what a unicorn looks like, but if your unicorn has a unique feature—let's say a pair of wings, or eyes that glow in the dark—you need to describe it in enough detail that your readers can picture it.

For example, in *The Last Olympian*, Percy and his comrades are confronted by a drakon, an ancient, dragonlike creature. Just saying, "and then Percy fought a drakon" isn't going to provide the reader with enough information or excitement. Rick Riordan paints a vibrant portrait of his beast:

> *We have drakon-fighting classes at camp, but there is no way to prepare yourself for a two-hundred-foot-long serpent as thick as a school bus slithering down the side of a building, its yellow eyes like searchlights and its mouth full of razor-sharp teeth big enough to chew elephants.*[3]

Because Riordan describes the drakon's size, eyes, and teeth, it is easy for the reader to imagine what it looks like and to appreciate the danger Percy faces. Remember to choose your words carefully so the unusual elements in your stories can be easily imagined by your readers.

Getting Your Descriptions Right

Ask your family and friends to help you practice your descriptive powers. Write a paragraph about a common animal, such as a cat or dog, without actually saying what it is, and see if your readers can guess. Try again with a more difficult animal, such as a leopard or grizzly bear, and ask if your descriptions are clear enough. Then, create an imaginary animal and ask your readers to draw a picture of it. Do their drawings match the image in your head? What changes can you make in your description to make it more lifelike for your reader? Do the same thing with a setting rather than an animal. Describe a common place, such as your living room, making sure to add lots of details without naming it. Then, try a more exotic location, or some place you've never been to but have read about.

Step 4

Write the Story

Just like playing sports, writing needs commitment and discipline. You'll need to write every day to improve and to achieve your goals. Set up a time every day to write and stick to it. It may seem strict, but it's the best way to get those blank pages filled. Look over your outline from Step 3 and estimate how long each section will take to write. Can you write a chapter every month? One short story every week? Grab your pencil or turn on the computer whenever inspiration strikes you, but keep to your scheduled time as well. There's a motivating writing program called National Novel Writing Month, for which authors sign up to write a 50,000-word novel during the month of November. It's a lot of work, but many people find it very rewarding. No one is expecting you to write an entire novel in just one month, but it's that sort of dedication that will help you finish your fantasy fiction.

Showing Versus Telling

An advantage of using the quest plot device discussed in Step 2 is that you can "show" rather than "tell" when it comes to describing your characters. During their journey, your characters will reveal their personalities if you have chosen the right tasks for them to perform. So rather than having to say, "Harry is a very considerate and brave boy," Rowling can demonstrate that he is through his actions. You can see this when Harry helps Viktor Krum save Hermione and rescues Fleur Delacour's sister during the underwater challenge in *Harry Potter and the Goblet of Fire*. Also, Harry's actions in the challenge show that he tends to act impulsively because he doesn't stop to remember that Dumbledore would never let the hostages drown. After the challenge is over, Harry scolds himself:

> *Harry's feeling of stupidity was growing. Now he was out of the water, it seemed perfectly clear that Dumbledore's safety precautions wouldn't have permitted the death of a hostage just because their champion hadn't turned up. Why hadn't he just grabbed Ron and gone? He would have been first back. . . . Cedric and Krum hadn't wasted time worrying about anyone else; they hadn't taken the mersong seriously.*[1]

Active Versus Passive

You've probably heard about using the "active voice" instead of the "passive voice." Basically, this means you want your sentences to be as forceful and direct as possible. Instead of saying "Green is a color that always pleases the girls," write "The girls love the color green." Make sure that the first part of your sentence is the most important part and that it is doing whatever the action [verb] is to the second part. The more active your writing is, the more involved your readers will be.

To be more "active," instead of writing "Josie was in a hurry because she was late," try something like "Josie raced down the side streets like a NASCAR driver to get to rehearsal on time." Note the imaginative use of verbs in this example from *The Last Olympian,* when Percy first sees the home of Luke's mother:

> *The front porch was infested with wind chimes. Shiny bits of glass and metal clinked in the breeze. Brass ribbons tinkled like water and made me realize I needed to use the bathroom.*[2]

Places are usually infested with bugs, not wind chimes, so this is an excellent way of painting a picture of how Percy perceives the many chimes. "Clinked" and "tinkled" are also wonderful verbs that give a vivid impression of Percy's experiences. Good writers always try to expand their vocabulary, so use your ideas journal from Step 1 to keep track of words you like, ones you learn, and ones you use too often. You want to paint a colorful portrait with your words, and the more imaginatively you use them, the better you will succeed. On the other hand, you don't need to spice things up purely for the sake of it. Saying things simply works, too, and prevents the reader from becoming tired of complicated descriptions or verbs that don't fit well.

Writing Dialogue

Dialogue is a very important part of your story. It's how the characters talk to one another, and it is also a way to get plot information to your audience. It needs to sound natural, like how real people talk. You need to balance it with the descriptive passages in which you describe landscapes, people, animals, etc.

Having long passages of only description or only dialogue can get boring for the reader. Dialogue is also a useful device for "showing, not telling," because how characters say things tells readers a lot about them.

How do you begin to write dialogue? First, think about what the goal of the passage is. Is your protagonist telling his or her friends about an important discovery? Is the villain confiding plans about a kidnapping to a sidekick? Are the parents having an anxious discussion about a hard decision? Having a general idea of why your characters are talking will help you get started.

Next, think about how your characters talk. If they are well educated, do they use big words? If they are shy, do they not speak very often? Someone who is impatient might speak rapidly, and someone who is angry might speak slowly. Finding a character's "voice" is a good way to develop his or her unique traits.

Vary the way that you write dialogue. Repetition can bore your readers. You don't want a long string of something like this:

Gus said, "I'm going with you to the hidden caves."
Charlotte said, "No, you're not."
Gus said, "But I really want to go."
Charlotte said, "You'll just be in the way."

If you alternate your words and choose them carefully, it will be more interesting for your readers. The passage listed above will be more exciting if it goes something like this:

"I'm going with you to the hidden caves," whispered
Gus anxiously.
"No, you're not," Charlotte insisted.
"But I really want to go," Gus whined.
Charlotte replied crossly, "You'll just be in the way."

Analyzing a Passage of Dialogue

Here is a brief conversation between Hagrid and Charlie Weasley, from *Harry Potter and the Goblet of Fire,* when Hagrid brings Madame Maxime to see the dragons that are being used for the first challenge in the Tri-Wizards Tournament:

> "I didn't know you were bringing her, Hagrid," Charlie said, frowning. "The champions aren't supposed to know what's coming—she's bound to tell her student, isn't she?"
>
> "Jus' thought she'd like ter see 'em," shrugged Hagrid, still gazing, enraptured at the dragons.
>
> "Really romantic date, Hagrid," said Charlie, shaking his head.
>
> "Four . . ." said Hagrid, "so it's one fer each o' the champions, is it? What've they gotta do—fight 'em?"
>
> "Just get past them, I think," said Charlie. "We'll be on hand if it gets nasty, Extinguishing Spells at the ready. They wanted

Although Gus and Charlotte say the exact same things, the way they say their lines of dialogue tells you how they are feeling and more about who they are. You could imagine from just those four lines of dialogue that Gus is Charlotte's younger brother. She thinks he's a pest, although he really wants to help her.

You need to be consistent when writing dialogue. You want Charlotte and Gus to sound the same way throughout your story, even as they grow and change. If Charlotte suddenly starts talking like a much older person, your readers will be confused.

> nesting mothers, I don't know why . . . but I tell you this, I don't envy the one who gets the Horntail. Vicious thing. Its back end's as dangerous as its front, look."[3]

Although it may look unimportant, readers are given lots of information here. We learn about the types of dragons, which one is the most dangerous, what type of security there is, fears about information leaks, etc. We also learn more about the personalities of the two people talking: Hagrid is more interested in fantastic beasts than romance; he and Charlie come from different areas, as indicated by the particular dialect each one speaks; and Charlie knows a lot about dragons. All these facts are imparted in just a few lines of dialogue. There are also good examples here of how to mix up the way that your characters sound. Are they tired, angry, afraid? Try coming up with different ways of saying "he said." Use such verbs as *sighed, shouted, cried, whispered,* etc. Think of all the different ways that people talk in real life and use them in your writing.

Harry Potter grows and learns new things throughout his years at Hogwarts, but he's still Harry. His "voice"—the way he talks and the types of things he says—remains the same.

Listen to your friends and family as they talk and consider how their "voice" reveals their personalities. It's helpful to think about the books researched in Step 2 and how the authors use dialogue. What plot points do they convey through description, and which through dialogue? What do you learn about their characters through the way that they speak? For example, the way that Professor Snape speaks to Harry tells the reader how he feels without J. K. Rowling's having to say, "Professor Snape hated Harry." And the fact that Hermione uses big words, while Hagrid does not, shows their different levels of education. The dialect Hagrid speaks tells you that he comes from a different part of England than Hermione does.

Crafting convincing dialogue is one of the most difficult aspects of writing. One way to get the hang of it is to write a descriptive passage first and then try to get the same information across by having your characters talk to one another. But remember to think carefully about your goals. Dialogue is great for showing how your characters relate to each other. It's not so good, though, for such things as telling your readers how a landscape looks.

 # Making Up Your Own Words

One fun way to grab a reader's attention in fantasy fiction is with a created language. In *Eragon,* Brom teaches Eragon the "ancient language"[4] so he can learn magic and communicate with special creatures, such as dragons and elves. The ancient language also helps teach Eragon the history of his home. After the first time Eragon has used magic, Brom explains to him:

> *Brisingr is from an ancient language that all living things used to speak. However, it was forgotten over time and went unspoken for eons in Alagaësia, until the elves brought it back over the sea. They taught it to the other races, who used it for making and doing powerful things. The language has a name for everything, if you can find it.*[5]

Listening to Dialogue

Using a book you researched in Step 2, choose some dialogue passages and read them aloud with your friends. How does the dialogue make the story move along? What do the conversations tell you about the characters? Do the characters talk like real people? How would you write it differently? After you've done this exercise with dialogue from other books, do it with your own work. Does the dialogue you've written sound the way you imagined? How can you strengthen it? What do your friends think?

You've probably seen examples of fantasy languages in the movies and on television, such as Na'vi in *Avatar*, the Elvish languages in the Lord of the Rings trilogy, or Klingon in *Star Trek*. Although it is fun, don't use it too often. If your readers are constantly wondering what your characters are saying, they'll get frustrated or bored quickly. It's a good idea to create a dictionary for yourself to keep your new language straight, and consider providing one for your readers as well. (Not an *entire* dictionary though—that would be a lot more work than even writing a fantasy novel! Just keep track of the new words you create so you and your readers don't forget what they mean.)

Or you could provide a glossary, like in the back of *Eragon,* for important words. As with all the elements you're using, be sure that there is a good reason for using a made-up language and that it adds to your story rather than distracts from it.

Editing Your Work

In addition to building your vocabulary, now is a good time to brush up on punctuation and grammar. And don't forget spelling! No one enjoys reading a book filled with spelling errors. Get help from a teacher, a parent, an older friend, or a librarian. Up to this step, you've been concentrating on your characters and your world and making them realistic. Now it's time to concentrate on the craft of writing. Go over your first drafts and view them critically, as if you were a stranger reading them for the first time. Edit for length so your story is as long as it needs to be but doesn't go on and on. Revise as needed, and then revise again. On Christopher Paolini's Web site, he says that he spent a year writing *Eragon* and then another year revising it.[6] The time he spent on editing *Eragon* is what helps make it such a fun book to read.

Adding Texture

To create a compelling world, you have to describe more than only how it looks. Just as you use all your senses every day, you need to include what your characters are hearing, feeling, tasting, and smelling. Close your eyes and listen to what is going on around you. If you described what you hear in writing, would your reader be able to guess where you are? Think of your favorite thing to eat and then write about it. Is it sweet or salty? Cold or hot? Crunchy or smooth? Does it have a strong scent that makes your mouth water when you smell it? These kinds of details will make your world more realistic and fun.

The following passage is from *Eldest,* the second in Paolini's Inheritance Cycle, and happens when Eragon visits a dwarf temple. After reading it, write something similar about what your protagonist experiences when he or she goes to a new place for the first time:

> *His first impression was of color. A burning-green sward splayed around the pillared mass of Celbedeil, like a mantle dropped over the symmetrical hill that upheld the temple. Ivy strangled the building's ancient walls in foot after foot of hairy ropes, dew still glittering on the pointed leaves. And curving above all but the mountains was the great white cupola ribbed with chiseled gold.*
>
> *His next impression was of smell. Flowers and incense mixed their perfumes into an aroma so ethereal, Eragon felt as if he could live on the scent alone.*
>
> *Last was sound, for despite clumps of priests strolling along mosaic pathways and spacious grounds, the only noise Eragon could discern was the soft thump of a rook flying overhead.*[7]

Step 5

What to Do With Your Finished Story

When Christopher Paolini self-published *Eragon,* he thought of a unique way to advertise his book: he traveled to more than 135 book stores and libraries while dressed as a medieval character.[1] His tactic helped spread word about his work, and eventually a big publisher reprinted his book. If you want to get your fantasy fiction published, you will also have to work very hard, and it may take a long time. There are lots of ways to try though, including online contests, blogs, self-publishing, and finding an agent. After you've done all your polishing and have asked family and friends to critique your story, it's time to make your work available to other readers.

Online Contests and Blogs

The Internet is a terrific resource and can be a big help to young authors. There are lots of ways to get your work noticed by people from all over the world. If you wrote some fan fiction in Step 2, post it online at a fan site and get some feedback. This is a good way to see how people react to your writing style and for you to get used to hearing your work critiqued by strangers.

Once you have a piece of writing that you really like, you might want to consider entering an online contest. The prize could be money or having your work published, but the main thing is to get your work out there into the world. Examine sites carefully before you submit your work, however. Make sure that the contests are free to enter and that you retain the rights to your work. It is a good idea to have your parents, a teacher, or another trusted adult look at each site with you. Be sure to follow the rules carefully. There's no point in entering the most awesome story ever if you don't follow the submission guidelines. Make sure that your work is formatted correctly, whether it is submitted electronically or through regular mail. Here are some places to start:

✔ The Amazing Kids Web Site offers contests for young writers, animators, and artists.

✔ Scholastic has an annual contest in its Kids Are Authors program that you can tell your teacher about. It's for kids in kindergarten to eighth grade, and although your teacher must organize it, it's a fun way to work with your friends.

✔ Amazon has a yearly contest for authors of full-length novels. Although the contest is not strictly for younger writers, there is a section for young adult fiction.

✔ A terrific resource is Kidpub, which has contests and also self-publishing. You can read works by other young authors and share yours.

✔ National Novel Writing Month has a young writers program that encourages young novelists to complete their works and find outlets for their publication.

Another avenue for getting your work read is your own blog. You can write about anything you like, post your fantasy fiction, and invite your readers to comment. Word Press has some useful, free software to help you get started. Blogging is a wonderful way to build your self-discipline by writing every day. Plus, you never know where it will lead; there have been people who have gotten book deals because of their entertaining, well-written blogs. Another place to go to learn about expressing yourself online is SparkTop. Again, be sure to check with the adults in your life before setting up your blog, and discuss privacy issues with them.

Self-Publishing

Self-publishing is exactly what you think it is: you publish your story yourself. You design the layout, the cover, and illustrations, then arrange for the book to be printed and distributed. The disadvantage of self-publishing is that you have to pay for it all, but then again, it is a way to get started. Paolini's parents were so impressed by *Eragon* that they self-published it when he was a teenager. After it caught the attention of famous author Carl Hiaasen, a big publisher purchased the rights to it.

Whether it's a thin paperback or a hardback with a beautifully illustrated cover, having your work published can be a big confidence booster. Check out CreateSpace, which helps you with the steps necessary for publishing on Amazon, your own Web site, or in book form. You'll also find articles about authors who have self-published and what the process was like for them.

Getting an Agent

A literary agent is someone who can help get your work noticed by a publishing company. He or she will read your work, evaluate it, get you an editor, and submit your story to different publishers. The agent will take part of what you get paid, but it will be worth it if your work gets published. Many publishing houses do not accept submissions from authors without agents. Finding an agent to represent you will not be easy, but stick with it, like you have done with your writing, and with some luck you'll get a good result. Be patient and be persistent. For lists of available agents, do some research on the Internet. Here are some places to start:

- ✔ WritersNet offers advice and listings from the Internet directory of writers, editors, publishers, and literary agents.

- ✔ The Association of Authors' Representatives has a searchable directory of literary agents.

- ✔ Science Fiction & Fantasy Writers of America has practical advice about what to look for in an agent and what to avoid.

After you've found some agents you might like to work with, you need to send them a "query letter," in which you tell them about yourself and your story. Make your letter entertaining and informative but also to the point. Agents are busy and appreciate short letters that grab their attention quickly. And remember, as former literary agent Durant Imboden says on his Web site, "Agents pay the rent and feed their families via commissions on manuscript sales. They aren't just looking for wonderful books; they're looking for wonderful books they can sell."[2]

You need to sell yourself and your manuscript. Stock up on supplies, such as good quality paper, envelopes with your return address, and stamps. Never sign a contract that calls for you to pay money up front, and never sign anything without letting your parents or a trusted adult read it first.

Get Some Feedback

Before you submit your work to an online contest or to a literary agent, it's important to get some feedback from people you trust. Show your finished story or novel to your friends, family, and teachers. Ask them to be specific about what they like or dislike. Emphasize the fact that you would like them to be honest and that you do not expect them to love every single little thing about your story in order to spare your feelings. They should really think about it. Do they find the characters believable? Does the dialogue flow? Did they enjoy the quest your characters were on? Do your descriptive passages give enough detail? Were your readers able to anticipate the ending, and did they feel that it fit the story? How do they feel about the length of your work? What would they change and why?

Remember, getting constructive criticism is extremely important for an author; without it, you cannot improve. Respond courteously to your readers, even if they aren't as positive as you'd like. You did ask for complete honesty, after all. Thank them for taking the time to help you. Keep a list of comments in your ideas journal so you know what to work on.

Stay Inspired

No one says that writing is always easy, but it is rewarding work that helps you grow as a person. It's fun, expands your imagination, and lets you experience things from other points of view. Writing fantasy is well suited to these goals. As Terry Pratchett, author of The Bromeliad Trilogy, said when he accepted the Carnegie Medal for the best children's book of 2001, "Fantasy isn't just about wizards and silly wands. It's about seeing the world from new directions."[3] The next step in your writing is up to you. You can write about wizards and wands (which are never silly), talking unicorns, futuristic societies, or anything that inspires you. As long as you tell *your* story with passion and originality, you will achieve something truly fantastic.

Chapter Notes

Step 1: Start With an Idea

1. "Biography," *J. K. Rowling Official Site*, n.d., <http://www
   .jkrowling.com/textonly/en/biography.cfm> (September 15,
   2011).
2. Ibid.
3. "Random Buzzers Q&A With Christopher Paolini—Part 3,"
   Shurtugal.com, November 16, 2010, <http://shurtugal.com/
   2010/11/16/random-buzzers-qa-with-christopher-paolini-
   %E2%80%93-part-3/> (September 15, 2011).
4. "The Author: About Christopher Paolini," *The Inheritance
   Cycle*, 2004, <http://www.alagaesia.com/christopherpaolini
   .htm> (August 13, 2010).

Step 2: Gather Story Elements

1. Philip Pullman, *The Amber Spyglass* (New York: Alfred A.
   Knopf, 2000), p. 13.

Step 3: Organize Your Story

1. Rick Riordan, *The Lightning Thief* (New York: Hyperion
   Books for Children, 2005), p. 11.
2. Cornelia Funke, *Inkspell* (New York: Scholastic, Inc., 2005),
   pp. 385–386.
3. Rick Riordan, *The Last Olympian* (New York: Disney
   Hyperion Books, 2009), p. 287.

Step 4: Write the Story

1. J. K. Rowling, *Harry Potter and the Goblet of Fire* (New York: Scholastic, Inc., 2000), p. 505.
2. Rick Riordan, *The Last Olympian* (New York: Disney Hyperion Books, 2009), p. 92.
3. J. K. Rowling, *Harry Potter and the Goblet of Fire* (New York: Scholastic, Inc., 2000), p. 328.
4. Christopher Paolini, *Eragon* (New York: Alfred A. Knopf, 2003), p. 140.
5. Ibid.
6. "The Author: About Christopher Paolini," *The Inheritance Cycle*, 2004, <http://www.alagaesia.com/christopherpaolini .htm> (August 13, 2010).
7. Christopher Paolini, *Eldest* (New York: Alfred A. Knopf, 2005), pp. 112–113.

Step 5: What to Do With Your Finished Story

1. "The Author: About Christopher Paolini," *The Inheritance Cycle*, 2004, <http://www.alagaesia.com/christopherpaolini .htm> (August 13, 2010).
2. Durant Imboden, "Getting an Agent to Say 'Yes,'" *Writing .org*, 2002, <http://www.writing.org/html/a_agents3.htm> (September 15, 2011).
3. "Pratchett Wins First Major Award," *BBC News*, July 12, 2002, <http://news.bbc.co.uk/2/hi/entertainment/2124520.stm> (July 18, 2011).

Glossary

compelling—Being very interesting and persuasive. A story is compelling if you are so interested in it that you can't put it down. A character is compelling if you can hardly wait to find out more about him or her.

consistency—If something is consistent, it is alike in its parts and makes sense as a whole, and there are no random or weird parts that jump out at the reader.

context—The environment or surroundings of your story. If your story is set in a circus, it would be within the context to have elephants and acrobats as characters.

conventions—The generally accepted rules governing a genre or character that have evolved over time. What "everyone knows" about the type of writing, character, or situation in question.

conviction—A firm belief in an idea or a person. To act with conviction is to act as if you really believe in what you are doing.

dialect—The type of language a person speaks, which can identify where he or she comes from geographically, how much education he or she has had, and the cultural group he or she identifies with.

first-person narration—Telling a story through one person's point of view, usually the protagonist. It is the "I" type of narration: "I visited my grandmother."

genre—A type or category of literature that has its own unique qualities separating it from others. Examples of genres are fantasy, romance, horror, mystery, and science fiction. Sometimes genres have similar characteristics, such as fantasy and science fiction, or fantasy and horror.

omniscient narration—Telling a story through an all-seeing, impartial narrator. It can describe the actions and feelings of different characters and is not told from one point of view: "Emily visited her grandmother."

plagiarism—Using work created by someone else without giving that person proper credit; taking another's work and saying it is your own.

plot device—An action, circumstance, or object that is used to make a story progress. The best plot devices flow naturally from the story and do not distract the reader.

point of view—The perspective from which a story is told. If we see an action through a particular character's eyes, we are seeing it from that person's point of view.

protagonist—The lead character in a piece of writing. The majority of the story is told about him or her. The protagonist is not necessarily a hero, as he or she does not have to be likeable or good. An antihero, someone for whom the reader does not feel sympathy, can still be the protagonist.

quest—A journey filled with adventure, usually to find a particular object or accomplish a specific goal, such as finding Horcruxes or becoming a Knight of the Round Table.

Further Reading

Books

Athans, Philip, and R. A. Salvatore. *The Guide to Writing Fantasy and Science Fiction: 6 Steps to Writing and Publishing Your Bestseller!* Avon, Mass.: Adams Media, 2010.

Hamilton, John. *You Write It: Fantasy*. Edina, Minn.: ABDO and Daughters, 2009.

Pope, Alice. *2011 Children's Writer's and Illustrator's Market*. 23rd annual edition. Cincinnati, Ohio: Writer's Digest Books, 2010.

Smith, Pamela Jaye. *The Power of the Dark Side: Creating Great Villains, Dangerous Situations, and Dramatic Conflict*. Studio City, Calif.: Michael Wiese Productions, 2008.

Strausser, Jeffrey. *Painless Writing*. 2nd edition. New York: Barron's, 2009.

Internet Addresses

J.K. Rowling Official Site

http://www.jkrowling.com/

Christopher Paolini's Inheritance Cycle

http://www.alagaesia.com/

Rick Riordan

http://www.rickriordan.com/home.aspx

Science Fiction & Fantasy Writers of America

http://www.sfwa.org/

Writers.Net

http://www.writers.net/

Index